Queen Elizabeth I

Queen Elizabeth I

By Robert Green

A First Book

FranklinWatts
A Division of Grolier Publishing
New York London Hong Kong Sydney
Danbury, Connecticut

Photographs ©: Art Resource: 39 (Bridgeman Art Library), 14, 22, 23, 38 (Giraudon); Corbis-Bettmann: 8, 9, 10, 36, 53, 56; Gamma-Liaison: 51 (Isabel Cutler); Library of Congress: 3, 26; North Wind Picture Archives: 6, 31, 41; Photo Researchers: 28; Reproduced by courtesy of the Trustees, The National Gallery, London: 48; Superstock, Inc. 34, 35 (Christie's, London), 25 (Collection of the Duke of Berwick & Alba, Madrid), 19, 30, 33, 55 (National Portrait Gallery, London), 42, 45; Topham Picturepoint: 13, 17, 21.

Library of Congress Cataloging-in-Publication Data

Green, Robert, 1969–
Queen Elizabeth I / by Robert Green.

p. cm.—(A First book)
Includes bibliographical references and index.
Summary: Follows the life of the strong-willed queen who brought new stability and vitality to England in the sixteenth century.
ISBN 0-531-20302-6

1. Elizabeth I, Queen of England, 1533–1603—Juvenile literature. 2. Great Britain—History—Elizabeth, 1558–1603—Juvenile literature. 3. Queens—Great Britain—Biography—Juvenile literature. [1. Elizabeth I, Queen of England, 1533–1603. 2. Kings, queens, rulers, etc. 3. Women—Biography. 4. Great Britain—History—Elizabeth, 1558–1603.] I. Title. II. Series.

DA355.G745 1997
942.05′5′092—dc21
[B] 96–51691
CIP
AC

Printed in the United States of America
1 2 3 4 5 6 7 8 9 10 R 06 05 04 03 02 01 00 99 98 97

Contents

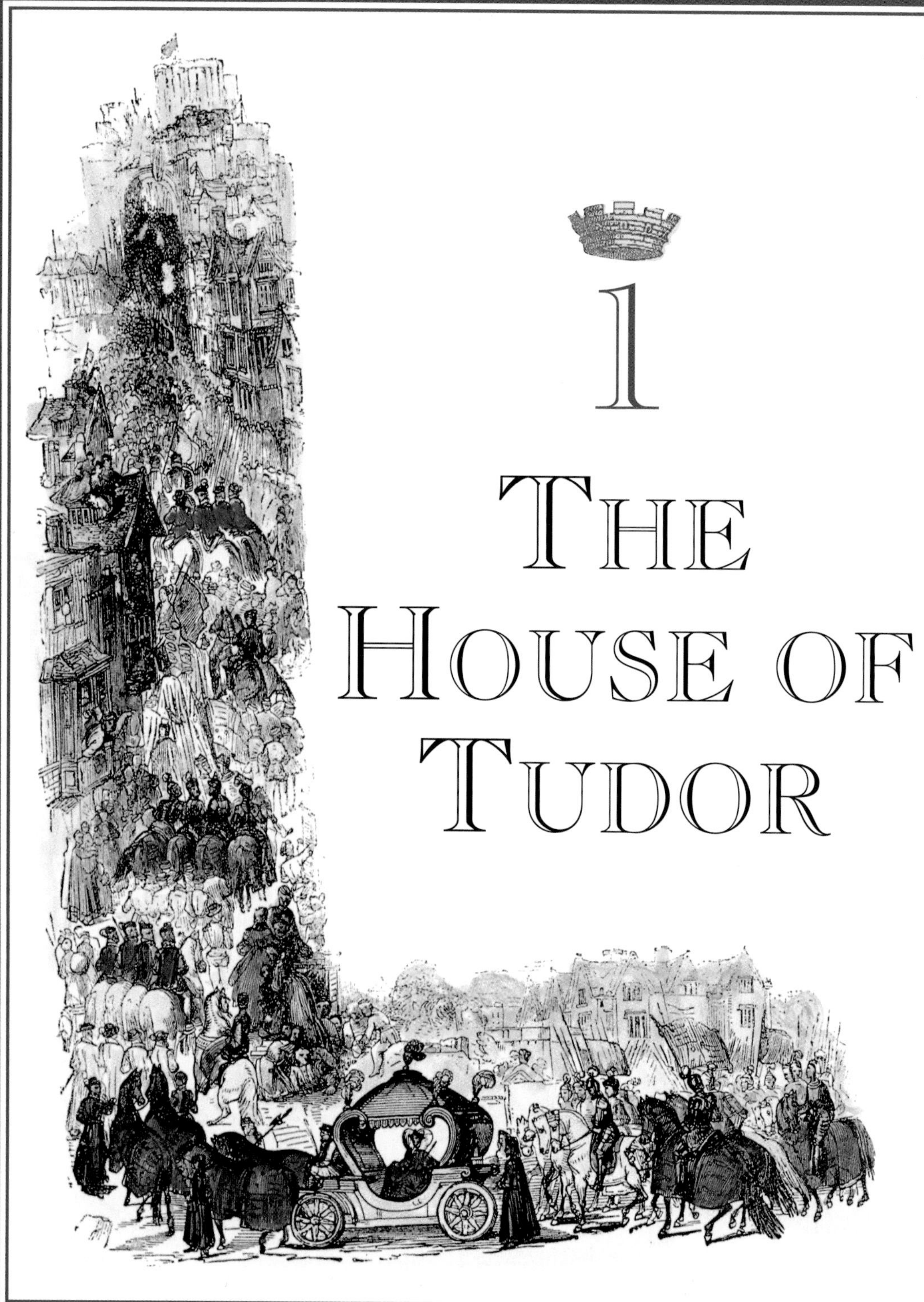

1

The House of Tudor

On November 17, 1558, Mary Tudor, Queen of England, died. But as the shouts of "The Queen is dead!" echoed in London's streets, the people had already taken up the new cry of "The Queen lives, God save the Queen." And as soon as arrangements had been made for the funeral of Mary, preparations were made for the coronation, or crowning, of Elizabeth Tudor, Mary's half sister.

Houses along the coronation route in London were given fresh coats of paint. The streets were lined with flags and banners. The people of London were anxious to learn what type of queen Elizabeth would be. Would Elizabeth, like Mary, bring England closer to Rome, where the pope headed the Catholic Church? Elizabeth had been forced to convert from Protestantism to Catholicism by Mary, but many believed that she was, at heart, still a Protestant.

In January of 1559, Elizabeth proceeded from the Tower of London to Westminster Abbey, where the rulers of England were crowned. Bells tolled from the church towers and bonfires blazed along the route.

During the procession, a young girl presented Elizabeth with a Bible in English translation. Reading the Bible in English instead of in Latin had been a crime punishable by death in Mary's Catholic England. But now Elizabeth kissed the book and held it high in the air for all to see. The Protestants in the crowd broke into jubilant cheers.

It was clear that Elizabeth would place England on a new path, a path toward religious reform and political independence. So successful was she that by the end of her reign, England had become a world power, and

Crowds gather to watch a Protestant being burned at the stake during the reign of Queen Mary. During this time, Elizabeth became a Catholic but secretly held her Protestant views.

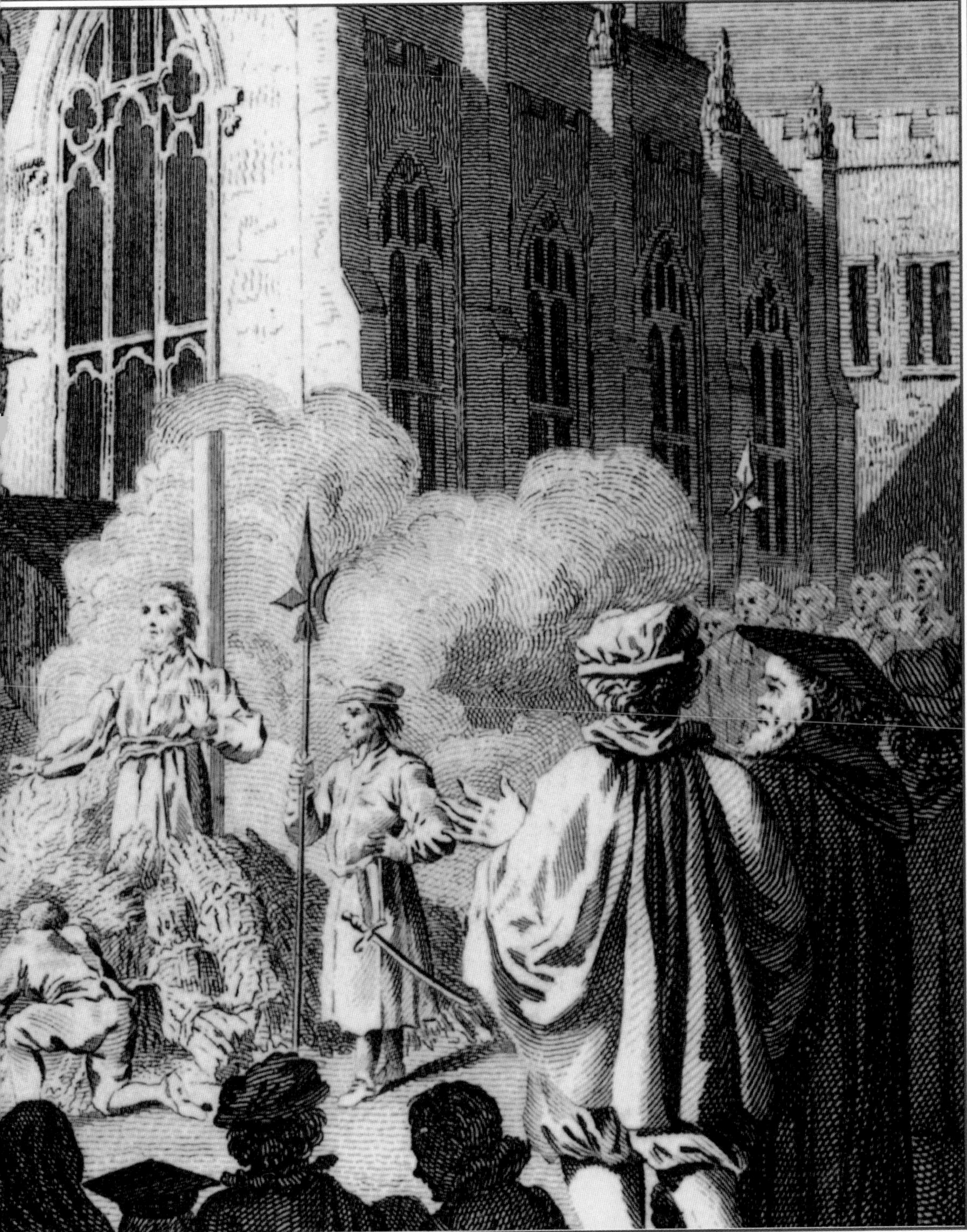

ENRICVS · VIII
ANG

she would be remembered as one of the most powerful monarchs in the history of England.

The crown of England passes from parent to child within a single family, called a dynasty. If a ruler did not have a child to succeed, the throne could fall to a distant cousin or it could be seized by another powerful family. Henry VII, who ruled from 1485–1509, was the first Tudor king, but it was his son, Henry VIII, Elizabeth's father, who brought glory to the Tudor name. Henry VIII fought hard against the two forces that could limit his powers: the nobility and the Catholic Church.

England was governed by the king and by the members of the two houses of Parliament. The seats of the upper house, the House of Lords, were filled by landholding nobles known as Lords. The seats of the lower house, the House of Commons, were filled by elected Englishmen who were not part of the nobility but came from wealthy families.

Parliament could influence the king in many ways. It advised him on important questions and voted on new laws. British monarchs at that time, unlike today, held real power and turned to Parliament just to approve policies. But Parliament also controlled the exchequer, or

King Henry VIII

treasury, of England. Parliament could therefore limit the king's powers by withholding money from him. Henry VIII, through force of character and through legislation, increased the powers of the king over Parliament and over the great land-holding nobility.

Henry VIII also limited the powers of the Catholic Church in England. The Catholic Church, headed by the pope in Rome, had grown to become the main religion in Europe. By Henry VIII's time, it was very rich and very powerful.

A movement had started in Europe, called the Reformation, to fight against the worldliness of the Catholic Church. Henry was angry that the Catholic Church tried to limit his powers, so he helped to bring the Reformation to England. He hated the fact that the English church obeyed the pope. Henry VIII was the king, and the king, thought Henry, should always be above the pope.

The brewing crisis between Henry and the pope boiled over when Henry wished to divorce his wife, Catherine of Aragon. Catherine had given Henry a daughter, Mary, but the king wanted a son to inherit the throne of England. Besides, he had his eye on a new

Catherine of Aragon, Henry's
first wife and the mother of Queen Mary

woman, Anne Boleyn. Henry appealed to the Church for a divorce, but the proceedings dragged on, and Henry became impatient.

In 1534, Henry decided to break from the Catholic Church. He proclaimed himself Supreme Head of the Church of England. The highest church official in England from that time on, under Henry, would be the Archbishop of Canterbury. All English citizens would owe allegiance to Henry as their king and as their spiritual leader. The Reformation in England was in full swing.

Henry divorced Catherine of Aragon and married Anne Boleyn. Anne gave birth to a daughter, Elizabeth, on September 7, 1533. But she also failed to give Henry a male heir. Henry had Anne beheaded and claimed that the marriage was invalid. Henry VIII would have six wives in all. His third wife, Jane Seymour, provided the king with a prince, named Edward, but the king went on marrying until late in his life.

Henry wrote the order of succession in his will. This would protect his children from the plots of ambitious nobles who might try to seize the throne. Edward was to succeed his father, then Mary, then Elizabeth.

Anne Boleyn, the mother of Queen Elizabeth, for whom Henry broke with the Catholic Church

Elizabeth was installed at the royal residence at Hatfield, where she grew very fond of her brother, Edward. She saw little of her father and appears not to have resented him for executing her mother. Each time Henry took a new wife, Elizabeth was brought to court to meet her new stepmother. But only with Henry's last wife, Catherine Parr, did she form a close bond.

Prestigious scholars were brought to Hatfield to tutor the princess. She zealously read ancient Greek and Latin and learned to speak French, Italian, and Spanish. Visitors to Hatfield were amazed by the child's ability to converse intelligently on complicated ideas, especially religion. Elizabeth was a devout Protestant.

After the death of Henry VIII in 1547, King Edward VI carried on the anti-Catholic reforms of his father. But Edward ruled briefly. He was never very healthy, and when he died in 1553, Mary succeeded him as their father had wished.

Under Queen Mary I, England's religious trend swung fully in the opposite direction. She married Philip, the Catholic king of Spain, and appealed to Rome for for-

Catherine Parr, Henry's sixth wife, created something of a home for Henry's three children and was the only stepmother that Elizabeth really knew.

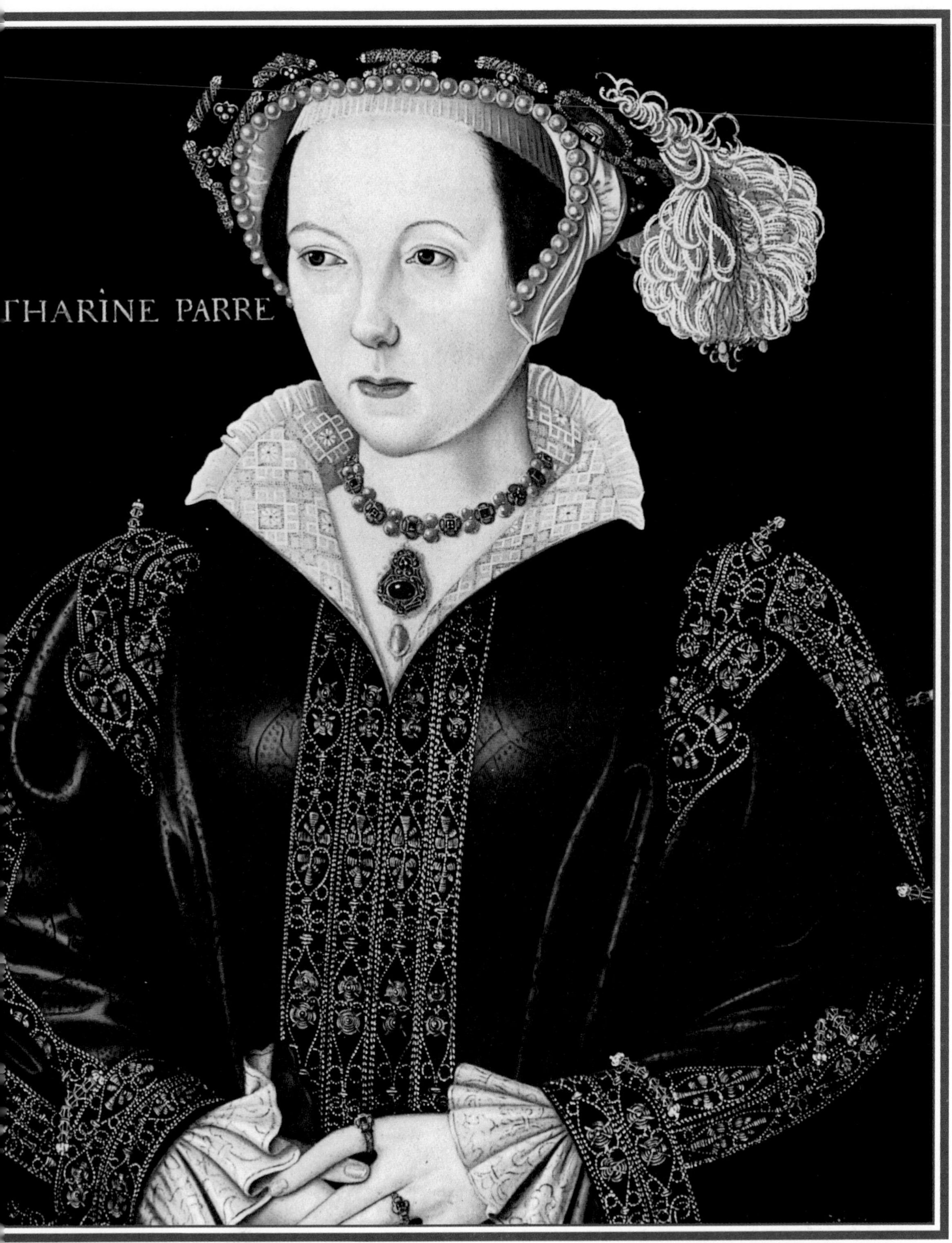
THARINE PARRE

giveness for what she considered to be her father's heresy. The reign of Mary was savage. She burned many Protestants at the stake and had many more beheaded. The people were soon calling her "Bloody Mary."

Mary's reign was, perhaps, the darkest and loneliest period of Elizabeth's life. She was forced to renounce her Protestant views under threat of death. Elizabeth was implicated more than once in plots to kill her sister. In March 1554, Mary locked Elizabeth in the Tower of London after a failed attempt at rebellion by Sir Thomas Wyatt. Though Elizabeth probably knew little of this plot, Mary considered executing her. Eventually, though, Elizabeth was allowed to return to Hatfield, where she was constantly surrounded by her sister's spies. Most of all, during these dark days, Elizabeth learned to hide her true feelings and bide her time until happier days came.

Fortunately for Elizabeth, Mary died on November 17, 1558, after ruling for only five years. Henry VIII had always wanted an heir who could match his own greatness, someone who would not give way to nobles or to the pope. Elizabeth now had her chance.

Queen Mary, known infamously as "Bloody Mary," married King Philip of Spain in 1554. The couple shared a fanatical hatred of Protestants, and Philip was recognized by the pope as king of England; the English, however, refused to recognize Philip as their king.

2

Conspirators and Suitors

When Elizabeth became queen of England, the kingdom and the throne were in a dangerous position. Great Britain was not then the unified country that it is today. Scotland was a separate kingdom ruled by Mary, Queen of Scots; Mary was Catholic and hostile to Protestant England. Wales, west

Elizabeth I's coronation portrait showing her with symbols of state

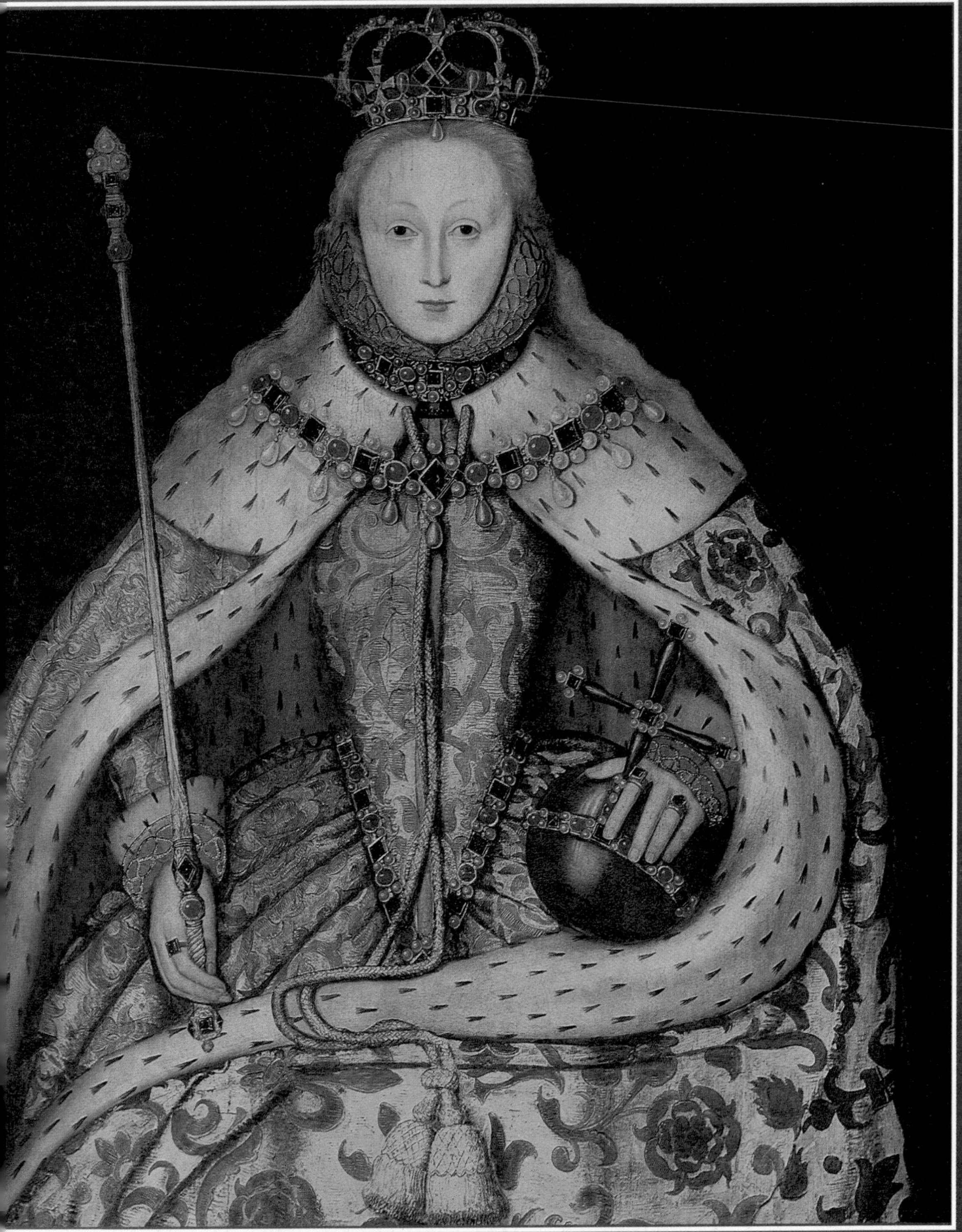

of England, was still a frontier. And Ireland, though nominally British, was in a state of rebellion—the Irish not only resented being ruled by a foreign power, but they remained largely Catholic.

It was unlike Elizabeth to move swiftly in matters of state—she loved to take her time mulling over her options. Once she became queen, however, Elizabeth quickly rid the Privy Council, her body of advisors, of Catholics. She replaced them with able men whom she thought she could trust. Chief among them was William Cecil (later Lord Burghley), who served Elizabeth faithfully throughout her reign, first as Secretary of State and then as Lord Treasurer.

Elizabeth then set out to make England Protestant again. In 1559, Parliament passed the Act of Supremacy, which proclaimed Elizabeth Supreme Governor of the Church of England. She made the Protestant church more accessible to the people. Services were spoken in English instead of Latin, and the Bible could be read in English.

Elizabeth demanded that certain important people swear an oath to the queen (above god) in order to prove their loyalty. Generally she was tolerant of privately held views, so long as public worship was restricted to legal displays. But for those who refused to conform to Elizabeth's religious reforms, the executioner waited.

Pope Pius V, head of the Catholic Church during the first half of Elizabeth's reign, considered Elizabeth a heretic.

Elizabeth lived in a time of political and religious violence, and her life was constantly threatened by plots and conspiracies.

The conflict with Rome worsened when Pope Pius V issued a denunciation, known as excommunication, of Elizabeth, the Pretended Queen of England and those heretics adhering to her." The pope went so far as to say that the assassination of Elizabeth by a Catholic would not be a sin.

In 1569, a group of Catholic earls stirred up a rebellion in northern England. They were savagely beaten down by forces loyal to the queen, but the threat had been real enough. In 1571, the queen's elaborate spy network detected an international conspiracy against Elizabeth known as the Ridolfi plot. Roberto Ridolfi, who came from a prominent Italian family, had been trusted by Elizabeth's government, but he became involved with discontented Catholics.

Both incidents, the rising of the northern earls and the Ridolfi plot, were linked to Mary, Queen of Scots. Although she was Elizabeth's cousin, Mary had grown up in Catholic France. She was an ardent Catholic, and her ties to France remained stronger than her ties to England. The Catholic Church considered Mary to be the rightful queen of England.

The French and the Spanish backed conspiracies to bring Mary to the throne of England. The conspiracies were uncovered by Sir Francis Walsingham, who was in charge of protecting the queen. Mary was imprisoned in the Tower of London, but Elizabeth did not want to punish her cousin too severely.

The discovery of the Babington plot in 1586, how-

Mary, Queen of Scots

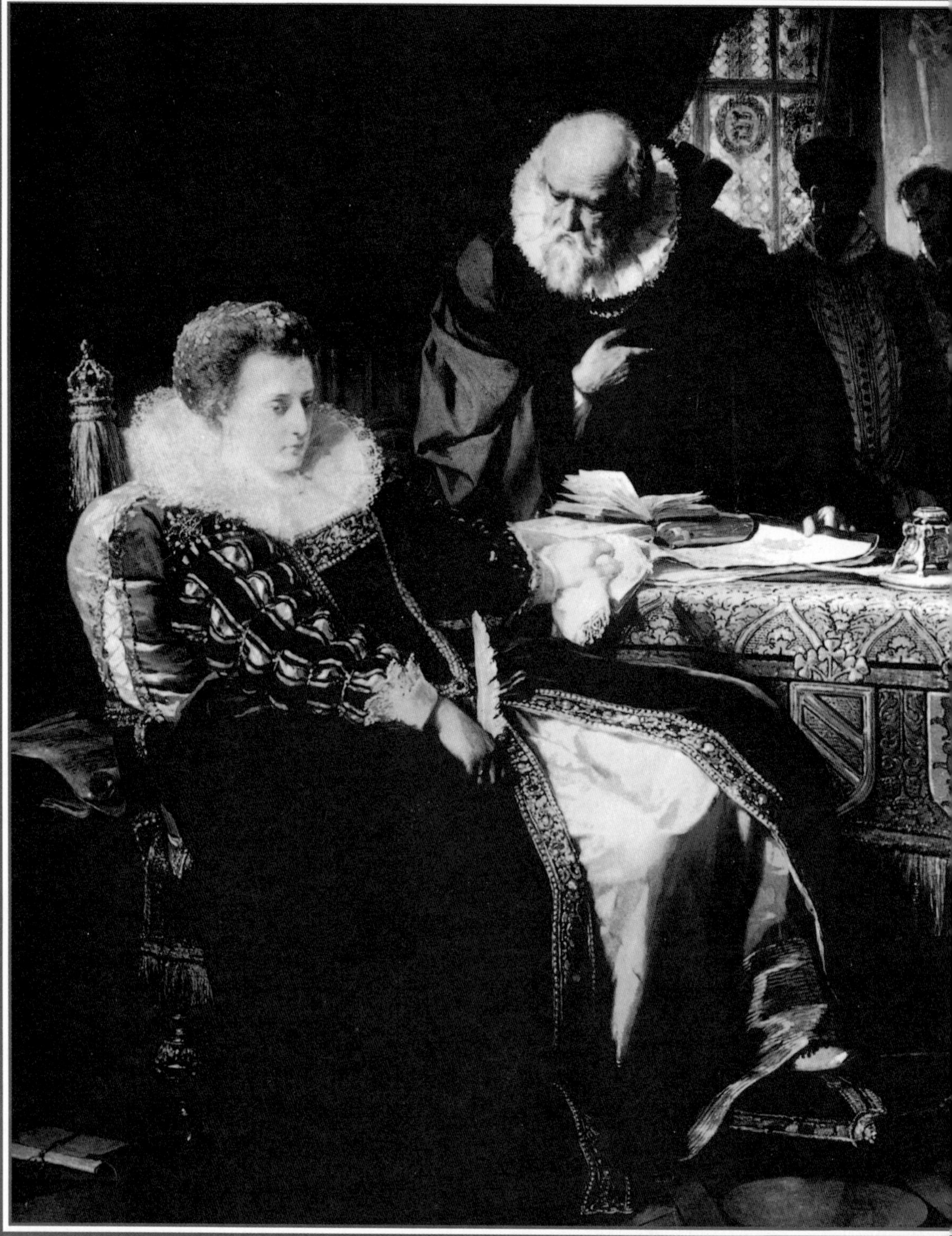

ever, sealed Mary's fate. Anthony Babington and Mary sent letters to each other about Babington's plan to murder Elizabeth and rescue Mary. Sir Walsingham intercepted the letters. Elizabeth would stand no more treachery from her cousin. In February 1587, Elizabeth had Mary beheaded.

The danger from Mary, Queen of Scots, had sprung partly from the fact that Elizabeth had no heir. When Elizabeth first took the throne in 1558, everyone tried to guess whom the queen would marry. King Philip II of Spain (the husband of her dead sister Mary) had offered early and been refused. King Erik XIV of Sweden, Archduke Charles of Austria, and Henry, Duke of Anjou (later king of France) were all turned down by Elizabeth, too.

There were many offers from Englishmen as well, including Robert Dudley, Earl of Leicester, the ambassador Sir William Pickering, and the Earl of Arundel. English society was still largely sexist, and Parliament reminded the queen that it was her duty to take a husband. But if Elizabeth married, she would lose some of her power, her independence, and her mystery.

"You have planned in divers ways and manners to take my life and to ruin my kingdom," Elizabeth wrote to Mary, Queen of Scots, shortly before she signed her death warrant on February 1, 1587.

Amid the opulence of Elizabeth's court, suitors competed to win Elizabeth's hand in marriage; all failed.

Besides, she liked men flirting with her, and her court was full of handsome courtiers. Elizabeth played one suitor against another and entered into prolonged marriage negotiations. But in the end all were rejected. Elizabeth proclaimed, "I am already bound unto a husband which is the Kingdom of England."

3

Courtiers and Privateers

Queen Elizabeth had proclaimed that she was married to the kingdom of England. To the people then, the queen was like a beloved mother. Whenever possible, she wooed her subjects with the language of love, preferring terms of affection over the usual heroic jargon of kings.

Portraits of Elizabeth were often done with politics in mind. She used paintings such as this one, portraying her as an angel of England standing over the map of Europe, to embolden her subjects and win their affections.

Queen Elizabeth was a marvelous talker. She spoke nine languages but was especially persuasive in English. She would coax and flatter Parliament and powerful nobles with beautifully turned sentences until she got what she wanted. When faced with opposition, however, Elizabeth drew herself up like a great peacock and unleashed violent tirades against the unlucky foe.

Elizabeth carefully created an image of elegance and majesty for herself. She sat amid her court in fantastically elaborate dress and draped in jewels. The ladies in her court were ordered to wear plain clothes to contrast the queen's splendor.

Being a woman proved to be an advantage for the queen; she wooed with charm and grace, while under-

Elizabeth at prayer, from a book entitled *Christian Prayers*, printed in 1569. The queen used her powers to compete with the Catholic Church and its dominance of Europe.

neath she had the iron will of her father, Henry VIII. The grandeur that all monarchs strive to achieve had much substance during Elizabeth's reign, for she stamped her age permanently with her image.

The Catholic European countries, to which England had historically looked for support, grew increasingly alarmed by Elizabeth's independence. In the 1560s and 1570s, France struggled with religious strife under two weak kings, Charles IX and Henri III. France was traditionally Catholic, but a sect of French Protestants, known as Huguenots, had rebelled against the Catholics.

Elizabeth pledged her support for the Huguenots; the French monarchs responded by denouncing her. But France was important to England, and Elizabeth entered into marriage negotiations with two French princes, the

Duke of Anjou and the Duke of Alençon, in order to bring the two countries closer. Elizabeth probably never intended to marry a French prince (and she never did), but by pretending to do so, she was drawing France away from Spain, which was becoming more and more dominant in Europe.

The Spanish had been pressuring France into a Catholic alliance, while in the Netherlands (Holland), the Dutch had been invaded by Spanish forces. The Dutch, who were largely Protestant, appealed to Elizabeth for military aid against the Catholic Spaniards.

After much negotiating, Elizabeth dispatched English forces led by Robert Dudley, Earl of Leicester, who was one of her favorite courtiers. But as the war in the Netherlands dragged on, Cecil reminded the queen that the Exchequer was nearly empty.

In 1580, the Spanish seized Portugal, their neighbor and fellow sea power. The wealth of Portugal helped Philip carry on his war in the Netherlands and build a great fleet of warships.

England desperately needed money. When Sir Francis Drake landed in England in September 1580 with a ship, the *Golden Hind,* loaded with Spanish treasure, Queen Elizabeth was delighted. Drake had just returned from a three-year voyage of privateering and treasure hunting; the Spanish were furious.

Sir Francis Drake, Elizabeth's favorite sea dog.

Spain, with its mighty galleons, had embarked on the creation of a vast overseas empire. After Christopher Columbus's voyage to the Americas for Spain's King Ferdinand and Queen Isabella, Spain had founded fabulously wealthy colonies in parts of Central and South America; they called this new territory the Spanish Main.

Spanish methods of colonization were cruel—they generally killed or enslaved the native populations and stole their resources. But Spain was able, with its newfound wealth and formidable navy, to become the strongest country in Europe.

Elizabeth watched as Spain grew rich, and she seethed with jealousy. Drake's family had suffered horribly in Mary's Catholic England, and he hated Catholic Spain. He offered to serve the queen in his pirate raids on Spanish shipping. In 1577, he set out to circumnavigate the globe and prey on the Spanish Main, the treasure house of the Spanish Empire, from the unguarded Pacific coast.

When Drake landed in England in 1580, he had not seen England for three years, he had lost four of his five ships, and most of his surviving sailors suffered from illness. He was uncertain how he would be received. But he need not have worried. The queen, although reprimanding him publicly for the benefit of the Spanish ambassador, privately congratulated him.

This early map of the Americas is from *Theatrum Orbis Terrarum,* the world's first regularly produced atlas. Notice that certain regions of the "New World" are labeled as territories claimed by European nations, such as "Nova Francia" ("New France") and "Hispania Nova" ("New Spain").

Drake's treasure helped to fill the coffers of the British Exchequer, and his sea charts gave England the key to the Spanish Main. The queen rewarded Drake with a knighthood and fondly nicknamed him her "Sea Dog."

For years, Queen Elizabeth had tried to avoid war with Spain. But now private English ships were frequently raiding Spanish treasure ships in the queen's name. Drake had started a craze. The Spanish ambassador complained, "at present there is hardly an Englishman who is not talking of undertaking the voyage, so encouraged are they by Drake's return."

The English had begun to find their sea legs. In 1583, Elizabeth appointed England's great captains—Sir Walter

Privateers in the 1500s combined the trades of piracy and commerce. They acted with the approval of their governments and often shared their stolen treasure with their sovereigns.

Raleigh, Sir Martin Frobisher, and Sir Francis Drake among them—to a new Royal Commission on the Navy. The commission prepared England for war, building new ships and gathering sea charts from the privateers.

In 1585, alarmed by England's intervention in the Netherlands and harassment of Spanish treasure ships, King Philip of Spain ordered the capture of English ships docked in harbors on the European continent. Elizabeth, who had always tried to avoid war, finally yielded to her hot-tempered advisors: Spain would have its war.

4

The Invincible Armada

It was in February 1587 that Elizabeth had beheaded Mary, Queen of Scots. This execution prevented King Philip of Spain from trying an invasion of England from Scotland. Instead, Philip planned an invasion of England by sea, a plan which came to be known in Spain as the "Enterprise of England."

Spanish inquisitors torture Protestants in this painting by Francisco Goya.

Flying the banner of Catholicism, Philip's Spanish Inquisitors had burned and tortured Protestants and supposed heretics all over Spain. Philip believed that he was winning God's favor by spilling the blood of non-Catholics. But England had emerged as an international threat to Catholic strength. Philip harnessed all the wealth of Spain to build an armada—a huge fleet of warships—that could crush Elizabeth's heretic kingdom and restore all of Europe to Catholicism.

Elizabeth got wind of Philip's armada preparations, and her great captains advised a first strike. Drake exclaimed, "give me a fleet and a free hand and I will smoke the wasps out of their nests." Elizabeth agreed, for once, on quick action, and she unleashed her Sea Dog.

Drake set out with twenty-four ships and nearly three thousand men for the Spanish port of Cádiz, where the Spanish Armada lay at anchor. Drake's fellow captains advised caution, but Drake sailed directly into

The hulking ships of the Spanish Armada, thought to be invincible

Cádiz harbor. By blocking the mouth of the bottle-shaped harbor, he corked the only escape route for the Spanish ships. His ships attacked. When he sailed out of the harbor again, thirty Spanish ships foundered in flames. Preparations for Philip's "Enterprise of England" had been set back at least a year.

Drake had struck quickly and then escaped. While the Spanish ships scoured the seas for him, he seized the treasure-laden *San Felipe* and towed his loot back to his grateful queen. Despite Drake's daring raids, the Armada was salvaged, and it left Spain on May 20, 1588.

The Duke of Medina-Sidonia, captain of the Armada, was to sail the 130 ships to a meeting with thirty thousand Spanish soldiers who had been fighting in the Netherlands under the command of the Duke of Parma. Philip also hoped that when the Armada crossed the English Channel, the English Catholics would join forces with them and rebel against Queen Elizabeth.

Elizabeth gathered her ships for the defense of England and appointed Baron Howard of Effingham Lord Admiral, commander of the fleet. But the inexperienced nobleman wisely relied on the low-born Francis Drake—who was appointed vice-admiral, or second-in-command—to command the fleet.

According to legend, when the Armada was sighted

The Ark Royal, the English flagship, led the English navy's defenses against the Spanish Armada. The red and white flags flying atop the fore and aft masts show the cross of St. George, the patron saint of England.

on July 19, 1588, Drake and Howard were occupied in a game of outdoor bowling near the port of Plymouth, where their ships awaited them. Drake, upon being told of the approach of the Spanish Armada, is said to have calmly replied, "We have time enough to finish the game and beat the Spaniards, too."

Some portraits of Elizabeth tell a story in small pictures. This painting, called the Armada Portrait, portrays the Spanish Armada in the upper left corner looking very strong, but in the upper right the Spanish ships are suffering a stormy defeat at the hands of the British. To emphasize the point, Elizabeth places her right hand on a globe to represent political domination.

Meanwhile, an army had been raised by the nobility to repel any Spaniards who might reach the English coast. The soldiers, under the command of the aging Earl of Leicester, gathered at Tilbury. The queen was invited to review her troops. She arrived at Tilbury on a white horse, dressed splendidly in white velvet and a silver breastplate. The Earl of Ormonde carried the sword of state before her, and a page carried a plumed helmet.

When the queen dismounted, the troops fell silent and she addressed the crowd:

> I know I have the body of a weak and feeble woman, but I have the heart and stomach of a king, and of a king of England too, and think foul scorn that Parma or Spain or any Prince of Europe should dare to invade the borders of my realm, to which, rather than any dishonour shall grow by me, I myself will take up arms, I myself will be your general, judge and rewarder of every one of your virtues in the field.

The soldiers were much cheered by Elizabeth's brave words, but in the end they would not be needed, for the battle would be won at sea. When Drake had finished their game of bowls, he and Howard led the English ships into the Channel. The Spanish ships outnumbered the English ships, but the English ships were faster and had longer-range cannons. The Spanish soon learned how hard it was to maneuver their massive hulks through the tricky waters of the English Channel with the English ships nipping at their heels.

After an indecisive day of fighting, the Spanish put in at the French port of Calais. Drake dismantled some of the smaller English vessels, set them on fire, and floated them into the anchored Spanish fleet. This simple trick cost the Spanish dearly, for many of the Armada ships could not evade Drake's fire ships and perished in flames.

When the Spanish ships reentered the Channel from Calais, they formed a crescent shape which was supposed to be invincible. The Spanish captains were used to grappling with other ships and boarding them with soldiers, resulting in a sort of land battle at sea. Instead, the English blasted away with their powerful guns, thus avoiding close contact with the Spanish.

On July 29, the English regrouped their forces and met the battle-weary Spanish in the Battle of Gravelines. The battle dragged on, as the English ships darted in and out of their native harbors for resupply. Finally, the crescent formation of the Armada broke and many Spanish ships sank. The English pursued the surviving Spanish ships northward, where many more were destroyed by

British ships venture into the Spanish Armada's crescent formation, which the Spanish believed could swallow the enemy. The English surprised the Spanish with the agility of their smaller ships, darting in and out of battle until the Spanish broke out of formation. The English did not lose a single ship.

savage winds. More than half of Philip's "invincible" Armada had been destroyed; the English had not lost a single ship.

England had won control of the seas, a prize they would hold for more than three centuries to come. Elizabeth greeted her people in the streets of London, and they expressed their devotion and gratitude. It may have appeared that the queen was experiencing her greatest moment, but matters of state weighed heavily on her. After the costly battle to defeat the Armada, the treasury was nearly empty.

Soon the queen received more bad news: the Earl of Leicester had died. He had once been the queen's favorite and had served her faithfully from the day of her accession. Leicester had been in command of the land forces against the Spanish invasion. He had not been needed because the Spanish never reached the English shore, and he knew that his days of glory had passed. The queen turned her attention to Leicester's dashing stepson, Robert Devereux, Earl of Essex.

5

Essex and After

Essex looms large in the last part of Elizabeth's reign. Though she remained unmarried, she never tired of flirting with her courtiers. When the Armada was defeated in 1588, Elizabeth was fifty-five years old. Her age was a sore point—no one dared mention it in her presence. She preferred to think of herself as a young queen still sought after by suitors.

In fact, she had not aged well. Her hair, long since gray, was covered with an auburn wig, and wrinkles were

clearly visible on her heavily painted face. But remarkably, she retained all the courage and will she had come to the throne with thirty years earlier. Her wit was still sharp and she kept a very firm grip on the throne.

The rash and courageous Earl of Essex, less than half the queen's age, must have reminded her of a time when her court swirled with bold men, all desiring her favor and flattering her with elaborate speeches. Essex was foremost a military man, long on courage and short on wisdom. He had served bravely in the campaigns against the Spanish in the Netherlands and against Catholic forces in France. But in these campaigns, he had also acted recklessly.

Cecil warned the queen about this young upstart and his refusal to obey orders. Essex was, in fact, Cecil's rival at court. With the help of the brothers Francis and Anthony Bacon, Essex maneuvered constantly to displace the influence that Cecil had over the queen. The queen liked Essex, but she was not ready to get rid of Cecil and his wise counsel.

Essex was angered by Elizabeth's refusal to appoint his allies, especially the Bacons, to high positions in her cabinet. Nevertheless, the queen allowed Essex to

Robert Devereux, Earl of Essex

command a war party against Spain. His bravery was undeniable. In the raid, the cities of Cádiz and Faro were sacked. But overall, the riches from the expedition fell short of the queen's expectations. Spain had been severely checked by the defeat of the Armada, but Philip found a more roundabout route to attack England—through Ireland.

Ireland had long been in a state of revolt. The rich, land-owning, Anglo-Irish lords retained soldiers to keep the Irish from throwing the English out. This is just the way Elizabeth would have preferred to keep things, for she had no money to send English troops. But the revolt continued to brew, and eventually English troops were dispatched.

In 1598, the Irish, under the command of Hugh O'Neil, Earl of Tyrone, dealt the English a major defeat at the Battle of Yellow Ford and killed the English commander. Tyrone proved to be a charismatic leader, and with guns and money supplied by King Philip of Spain, he threatened to drive the English out of Ireland entirely.

The D'Arcy Castle, Clifden, Ireland; after the defeat of the Spanish Armada, Philip II of Spain tried again to attack the English, but this time in English-occupied Ireland.

Elizabeth was determined to avenge the defeat. She put Essex in command of the English army in Ireland and told him not to return until he had defeated Tyrone. It was an enormous gamble for Essex. On the one hand, he could finally win great military fame. On the other hand, if he failed he would be ruined.

Essex floundered. He marched the English forces around Ireland until the army was cut in half by disease, starvation, and desertion. The queen sent off angry letters ordering him to attack Tyrone in his northern stronghold of Ulster. When Essex finally met Tyrone in Ulster, he negotiated a truce and then hurried back to England to throw himself on the queen's mercy.

Essex had clearly lost his gamble. His sudden appearance in England enraged the queen. She replaced him with Lord Mountjoy, who defeated Tyrone and five thousand Spanish reinforcements in 1601. Essex felt himself gravely wronged and took up arms against the queen herself.

Essex had hoped for an uprising in London to help press his claims against the queen. The people had little sympathy for him, though, and he was arrested in 1601 and, on Elizabeth's orders, executed for treason.

Though no monarch in that era of British history was safe from rebellion among the nobility, the common

A View of the House of Peers, Queen Elizabeth on the Throne, the Commons attending.
Taken from a Painted Print in the Cottonian Library.

Elizabeth presides over a session of the House of Lords with members of the House of Commons looking on.

people were very fond of Elizabeth. The House of Commons had been increasing its power over the House of Lords, and new social legislation was being passed. Perhaps the most important new law was the Poor Law of 1601, in which the government recognized the need to supply minimum living standards to everyone and levied taxes to pay for relief programs for the poor.

The queen was quite old by then, "a lady surprised by time," as Sir Walter Raleigh put it. The war with Philip had plagued her reign, and, in fact, would outlive her. England was still short of money; in 1601, Parliament pressed her to repeal the monopolies on profitable trades that she had awarded to loyalists.

But Elizabeth still knew how to handle Parliament. Glittering with jewels and topped by her red wig, she delivered what came to be known as her "Golden Speech": "There is no jewel, be it of never so rich a prince, which I set before this jewel: I mean your love." Once again Elizabeth won the affection of her ministers, but she was forced to concede on the monopolies.

She had become a legend and an institution in her own time. She was called "Gloriana" and "the Virgin Queen" by poets and "the great lioness" by people in the streets.

Elizabeth resisted aging with all the cosmetics of her day. By the end of her life she must have presented a gaudy spectacle: her face coated with thick powders, her hair dyed to preserve its reddish hue, and gems and pearls hanging in her clothes and hair. She was "a woman surprised by time," reported one observer. Nonetheless, she died gracefully, "as easily as a ripe apple from a tree."

William Shakespeare recites his play *Macbeth* before the court of Queen Elizabeth. Elizabeth, skilled in her own right at delivering a well-turned phrase, rejoiced in the literary achievements of the Elizabethan Age.

Even in 1603, seized by sickness and close to death, Elizabeth would not give up her authority. Although gripped with fever, she refused to rest. Robert Cecil, fearful that the queen would collapse, pleaded, "Madam, to content the people you must go to bed." "Little man, little man," Elizabeth flashed back, "the word *must* is not to be used to princes." And on March 24, 1603, Queen Elizabeth I of England died, leaving no immediate successor. (Mary Stuart's son became the next ruler of England, James I.)

With the death of Elizabeth, the Tudor dynasty came to an end. But she left England with a new system of government and a new religion. Her father, Henry VIII, had loosened the chains of Rome, and Elizabeth had buried them.

Moreover, Elizabeth had defeated rival claims to the throne and guided England's victories over the Spanish Armada and over Tyrone's rebellion in Ireland. She had, in short, helped create a wave of nationalism that strengthened feelings of unity among the English.

Elizabeth's independence and secular attitudes had another welcome effect: a flourishing of the arts. Painters and poets were as common to her court as dukes and earls. It was the age of John Donne and Edmund Spenser, of Christopher Marlowe and the early writings of William Shakespeare, and of the essays of Francis Bacon that caused such a stir in London. So devoted was the queen to her poets, and the poets to their queen, that their great age of creativity is known simply as the Elizabethan Age.

For More Information

Duncan, Alice Smith. *Sir Francis Drake and the Struggle for an Ocean Empire.* New York: Chelsea House, 1993.

Hibbert, Christopher. *The Virgin Queen: Elizabeth I, Genius of the Golden Age.* Reading, Mass.: Addison-Wesley, 1991.

Shakespeare's England. New York: M. Cavendish, 1989.

Stepanek, Sally. *Mary, Queen of Scots.* New York: Chelsea House, 1987.

For Advanced Readers

Cannon, John and Ralph Griffiths. *The Oxford Illustrated History of the British Monarchy.* New York: Oxford University Press, 1989.

A Portrait of Elizabeth I: In the Words of the Queen and Her Contemporaries. Edited by Roger Pringle. London: Ward Lock Educational, 1980.

Ross, Stewart. *Elizabethan Life.* North Pomfret, Vt.: Trafalgar Square, 1991.

Saraga, Jessica. *Tudor Monarchs.* North Promfret, Vt.: Trafalgar Square, 1991.

Strachey, Lytton. *Elizabeth and Essex.* New York: Harvest Books, 1969.

Internet Sites

Due to the changeable nature of the Internet, sites appear and disappear very quickly. Internet addresses must be entered with capital and lowercase letters exactly as they appear.

The Yahoo directory of the World Wide Web is an excellent place to find Internet sites on any topic. The directory is located at:

http://www.yahoo.com

This Web site contains a biography of Elizabeth I, works by and about the queen, and links to many different sources:

http://www.alchemyweb.com/~alchemy/englit/renlit/eliza.htm

Another site on Elizabeth I contains a chronology of her reign, a list of members of her court, and additional links to related sites:

http://www.interstudio.co.uk/users/ha26/

Many Web sites and search engines provide information and links on broader topics in history. One example is a Web page called History Resources, a guide to a huge variety of history sites:

http://www.liv.ac.uk/~evansjon/humanities/history/history.html

Kings and Queens of England and Great Britain with Years of Reign

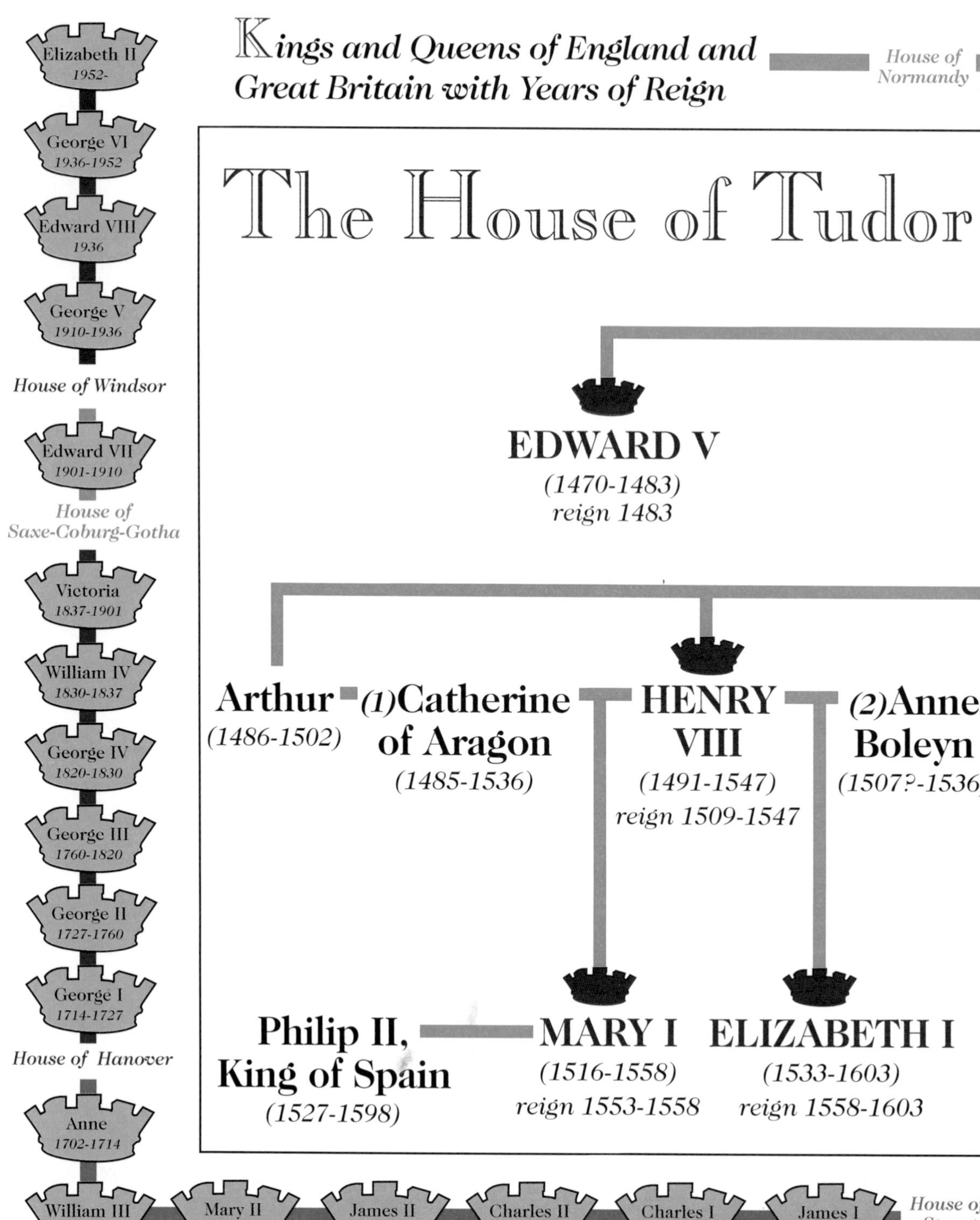
House of Normandy
The House of Tudor
EDWARD V
(1470-1483)
reign 1483
Arthur
(1486-1502)
(1)Catherine of Aragon
(1485-1536)
HENRY VIII
(1491-1547)
reign 1509-1547
(2)Anne Boleyn
(1507?-1536)
Philip II, King of Spain
(1527-1598)
MARY I
(1516-1558)
reign 1553-1558
ELIZABETH I
(1533-1603)
reign 1558-1603
Elizabeth II
1952-
George VI
1936-1952
Edward VIII
1936
George V
1910-1936
House of Windsor
Edward VII
1901-1910
House of Saxe-Coburg-Gotha
Victoria
1837-1901
William IV
1830-1837
George IV
1820-1830
George III
1760-1820
George II
1727-1760
George I
1714-1727
House of Hanover
Anne
1702-1714
William III
1689-1702
Mary II
1689-1694
James II
1685-1688
Charles II
1660-1685
Charles I
1625-1649
James I
1603-1625
House of Stuart

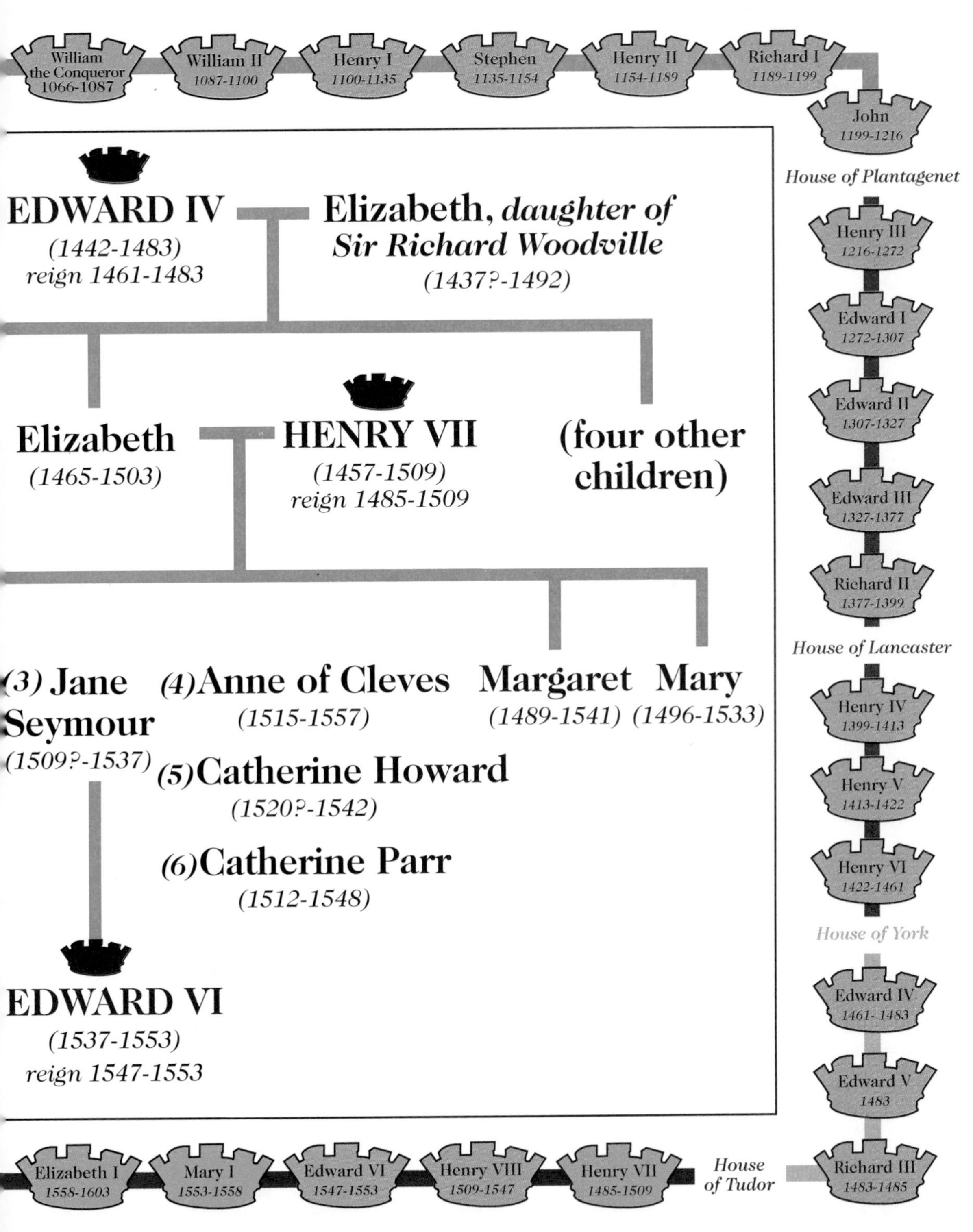

William the Conqueror 1066-1087
William II 1087-1100
Henry I 1100-1135
Stephen 1135-1154
Henry II 1154-1189
Richard I 1189-1199
John 1199-1216
House of Plantagenet
Henry III 1216-1272
Edward I 1272-1307
Edward II 1307-1327
Edward III 1327-1377
Richard II 1377-1399
House of Lancaster
Henry IV 1399-1413
Henry V 1413-1422
Henry VI 1422-1461
House of York
Edward IV 1461- 1483
Edward V 1483
Richard III 1483-1485
House of Tudor
Henry VII 1485-1509
Henry VIII 1509-1547
Edward VI 1547-1553
Mary I 1553-1558
Elizabeth I 1558-1603
EDWARD IV
(1442-1483)
reign 1461-1483
Elizabeth, daughter of Sir Richard Woodville
(1437?-1492)
Elizabeth
(1465-1503)
HENRY VII
(1457-1509)
reign 1485-1509
(four other children)
(3) Jane Seymour
(1509?-1537)
(4) Anne of Cleves
(1515-1557)
(5) Catherine Howard
(1520?-1542)
(6) Catherine Parr
(1512-1548)
Margaret
(1489-1541)
Mary
(1496-1533)
EDWARD VI
(1537-1553)
reign 1547-1553

Index

Page numbers in *italics* refer to illustrations.

About the Author

Robert Green is a freelance writer who lives in New York City. He is the author of *"Vive la France": The French Resistance during World War II* and biographies of important figures of the ancient world: *Alexander the Great, Cleopatra, Hannibal, Herod the Great, Julius Caesar,* and *Tutankhamun,* all for Franklin Watts. He has also written biographies of Queen Elizabeth II and King George III.